Darrell Miles
and
William Bigley

QUANTITY COOKING

Tested Recipes for Twenty or More

Dover Publications, Inc.
New York

Copyright © 1976 by Dover Publications, Inc.
All rights reserved under Pan American and International Copyright Conventions.

Published in Canada by General Publishing Company, Ltd., 30 Lesmill Road, Don Mills, Toronto, Ontario.
Published in the United Kingdom by Constable and Company, Ltd., 10 Orange Street, London WC 2.

This Dover edition, first published in 1976, is a corrected republication of *Dare to Excel in Cooking. Award Winning Group Recipes of "USS Semmes" (DDG-18)*, published by the United States Government Printing Office in 1966. This book contains a new publisher's note, incorporating information in the original forewords.

International Standard Book Number: 0-486-23318-9
Library of Congress Catalog Card Number: 75-46351

Manufactured in the United States of America
Dover Publications, Inc.
180 Varick Street
New York, N. Y. 10014

PUBLISHER'S NOTE

These recipes, originally prepared for use on the USS SEMMES (DDG-18), were part of that ship's entries in a competition among navy messes, the Ney Memorial Awards. Established as an annual all-Navy food-service competition, the awards give recognition to outstanding accomplishment in the preparation, service and management of food within the U.S. Navy.

When the USS SEMMES became a finalist in the 1966 competition, this cookbook was prepared in response to many requests for the acclaimed recipes. Just before publication of the book, the Secretary of the Navy announced that the SEMMES had won the trophy for the outstanding small mess afloat.

Table of Contents

Part One

Soups

CORN CHOWDER

(yield 25, 1 cup portions or 6¼ qts)

½ lb bacon
1 cup chopped onions
5 #303 cans whole grain corn
7 cups corn liquid plus ham stock or water
4 tbsp chopped celery

4 tbsp chopped green peppers
1½ cups potatoes, cut in ½ inch cubes
1 tbsp & 1½ tsp salt
1½ tsp pepper
6¼ 14 oz cans evaporated milk

1. Cook bacon over medium heat until lightly browned.

2. Add onions, cook until onions are transparent, stirring occasionally.

3. Drain corn; set aside for use in step 6.

4. Stir liquid (corn liquid plus ham stock or water) into onion mixture.

5. Add potatoes, celery, and green peppers. Cover and simmer approximately 15 minutes or until vegetables are tender.

6. Add drained corn, salt, pepper, and milk. Heat thoroughly before serving, stirring frequently.

7. Garnish with chopped parsley.

Note: 5 # 303 cans, cream-style corn may be substituted for the whole grain corn in step 3. Substitute water for the corn liquid in step 4.

VARIATION

1. MEATLESS CORN CHOWDER: Substitute 2 tbsp shortening for the bacon in step 1. Omit ham stock in step 4.

MINESTRONE SOUP

(yield 25, 1 cup portions or 6¼ qts)

¾ cup dry kidney beans
1¼ gal beef stock
1 bay leaf
1 tbsp & 2 tsp salt
1 tsp pepper
½ lb diced bacon
1 garlic clove, minced
2 cups chopped onions
3 cups shredded cabbage
1½ cups chopped carrots

1½ cups chopped green beans
1½ cups diced raw potatoes
½ lb chopped raw spinach
1½ cups diced celery
¼ cup chopped parsley
2 #303 cans tomatoes
½ cup spaghetti
½ cup sifted flour
¾ cup cold water

1. Cook dry beans according to directions on package.

2. Add stock, bay leaf, salt, and pepper. Simmer for 30 minutes.

3. Sauté garlic and onions with bacon until bacon is browned and crisp. Drain.

4. Add bacon, garlic, onions, cabbage, carrots, beans, potatoes, spinach, celery, parsley, tomatoes, and spaghetti to soup stock. Simmer approximately 45 minutes.

5. Blend flour and water to a smooth paste; stir into soup and cook 10 minutes longer.

CONSOMME

(yield 25, 1 cup portions or 6¼ qts)

6 lbs diced beef
2 tbsp shortening
2¼ qts cold water
2 tbsp salt
3 lbs cracked veal bones (optional)
2 tbsp shortening
½ cup ½ inch carrot cubes
1¼ cups chopped celery, including tops

2 cups chopped onions
¾ cup diced turnips
1 bay leaf
¾ tsp ground cloves
⅛ cup chopped fresh parsley
1½ tsp pepper
1¼ tsp thyme

1. Cut meat into 1 inch cubes. Cook in hot, melted shortening until brown.
2. Add water, salt, and veal bones. Heat to boiling temperature. Cover, reduce heat, and simmer for one hour.
3. Melt additional shortening, add carrots, celery, onions, and turnips. Sauté for 10 minutes.
4. Combine sauteed vegetables, bay leaf, cloves, parsley, pepper, thyme and stock Cover and simmer for 3 hours. Add hot water as needed. Do not stir.
5. Strain through double layer of cheese cloth. Skim off any excess fat.
6. Serve hot.

VARIATION

CONSOMME MAGENTA: Just before serving, add 1½ cups of tomato juice and ⅔ cup of finely chopped fresh parsley to clear consomme.

CREAM OF POTATO SOUP

Using instant mashed potatoes

(yield 25, 1 cup portions or 6¼ qts)

2 tbsp salt
6 cups chopped onions
1 lb finely diced bacon
2¼ cups dry, nonfat, milk

5¼ qt warm water
1 qt cold water
2¼ cups instant mashed potatoes
1½ tsp pepper

1. Chop onions and set aside for use in step 2.
2. Sauté bacon until lightly browned, add onions and continue sauteing until onions are transparent. Drain, set aside for use in step 4.
3. Sprinkle nonfat milk on warm water, stirring gently until almost dissolved. Allow to stand 15 minutes.
4. Add bacon and onions, bring just to a boil. Remove from heat.
5. Add cold water to milk mixture.
6. Combine potato granules, salt, and pepper.
7. Add to milk mixture, stirring constantly. Bring just to boiling point. Reduce heat and simmer 15 minutes.

Part Two

Salads

and

Salad Dressings

BANANA SALAD

(yield 25, ½ Banana Portions)

12 bananas, A. P.*
½ cup evaporated milk
1½ cups mayonnaise

5 cups shredded coconut
3 qts shredded lettuce

1. Peel bananas. Cut in half crosswise.
2. Add milk to mayonnaise. Dip each half banana in mixture. Roll in coconut.
3. Put shredded lettuce about ½ inch thick on baking sheet.
4. Place coated bananas about 2 inches apart on lettuce.
5. Serve well chilled.

* See part 9

PINEAPPLE CHEESE SALAD

(yield 25, ½ cup portions or 3¼ quarts)

2 #2½ cans pineapple chunks or tidbits
3 qts coarsely cut lettuce
½ cup salad dressing

2½ cups shredded natural cheddar cheese
pimiento strips—to garnish

1. Drain pineapple well. Save the juice.
2. Lightly mix together lettuce, cheese, and pineapple.
3. Cover with waxed paper. Store in refrigerator to chill thoroughly.
4. Blend in salad dressing just before serving.
5. Garnish with pimiento strips.

PICKLED GREEN BEANS

(yield 25, ½ cup portions)

1 #10 can or 4 #2½ cans drained,
   green beans
½ qt finely chopped onions
½ garlic clove, finely chopped
1½ cups vinegar
½ cup salad oil
2 tbsp prepared horseradish

4 tbsp sugar
½ tsp salt
¼ tsp allspice
½ tsp dry mustard
¼ tsp ground cloves
1 tsp celery seed

1. Toss beans lightly with onions and garlic.
2. Combine vinegar and oil. Add horseradish, sugar, and seasonings. Pour over beans.
3. Bring to a boil and simmer 5 minutes.
4. Cover container and place in refrigerator to chill thoroughly before serving.

STUFFED CELERY STICKS
(yield 25, 1 stalk portions)

25 pieces celery, A.P.*
½ lb. cheddar cheese
4 tbsp green peppers (optional)
4 tbsp sweet pickle relish

pinch cayenne pepper
½ tsp salt
paprika to garnish

1. Clean celery, place in ice water until crisp. Do not remove crisp leaves.
2. Grind cheese and green peppers. Combine with remaining ingredients and beat in mixer on low speed until creamy.
3. Remove celery from water. Drain.
4. Spread 1¼ tablespoons cheese mixture in hollow of each piece of celery.
5. Sprinkle paprika lightly on each piece to garnish, if desired.
6. Cover with waxed paper and store in refrigerator to chill before serving.

Note: Pimiento may be added in place of green peppers.

* See Part 9

MACARONI SALAD
(yield 25, ¾ cup portion)

5 cups elbow macaroni, A.P.*
5 qt. boiling water
1¼ tbsp salt
2 cups finely chopped onions
½ cup finely chopped green peppers
½ cup finely chopped pimiento

2¼ tsp celery salt
5 chopped, hard cooked eggs
1¾ cups chopped sweet pickles
½ lb. cheddar cheese, ¼ inch cubes
3 cups salad dressing

1. Cook macaroni according to instructions on package. Drain thoroughly. Chill.
2. Combine onions, green peppers, pimiento, eggs, and celery salt with chilled macaroni.
3. Fold in pickles, cheese,and salad dressing. Toss lightly until well mixed.
4. Cover with waxed paper. Store in the refrigerator to chill thoroughly before serving.

* See part 9

CARROT SALAD
(yield 25, ¾ cup portions or 5½ qts)

1 gal ground carrots
½ gal diced celery
½ qt mayonnaise
½ tsp salt

1 tbsp sugar
½ cup + 2 tbsp evaporated milk
1 tbsp lemon juice (optional)

1. Combine carrots and celery.
2. Combine milk, mayonnaise and seasonings; add to vegetables.
3. Toss together lightly. Cover with waxed paper and store in refrigerator to chill before serving.

COLD POTATO SALAD
(yield 25, ¾ cup portions)

3 qts cooked cold potatoes
5 tbsp salad oil
2 tbsp vinegar
1 tbsp prepared mustard
1⅛ tsp sugar
2 tbsp salt
¼ tsp pepper
pinch cayenne pepper
2½ cups finely diced celery

1 cup finely chopped onions
½ cup finely chopped green peppers
¾ cup sweet pickle relish
8 chopped, hard cooked eggs
3 tbsp finely chopped pimiento
1½ cups salad dressing
chopped parsley to garnish
paprika to garnish

1. Dice cold potatoes into ½ inch cubes.

2. Mix oil, vinegar, prepared mustard, sugar, salt, pepper and cayenne pepper. Pour over potatoes; allow to marinate for 15 minutes.

3. Combine celery, onions, green pepper, pickle relish, hard cooked eggs, pimiento, and salad dressing with diced potatoes. Mix lightly but thoroughly.

4. Sprinkle top with parsley and paprika.

5. Cover with waxed paper and store in refrigerator to chill well before serving.

CHICKEN SALAD
(yield 25, ¾ cup portions or 1¼ gal)

2½ qt well chilled, cooked chicken
12 chopped, hard cooked eggs
2½ qt diced celery
1¾ tbsp salt

½ tsp pepper
6 tbsp chopped pickles
1 cup mayonnaise

1. Cut chicken into ½ inch cubes.

2. Add eggs, celery, salt, pepper, pickles, and mayonnaise to chicken. Mix well.

3. SERVE IMMEDIATELY OR COVER WITH WAXED PAPER AND STORE IN THE REFRIGERATOR.

Note: Serve on lettuce.

VARIATION

PINEAPPLE AND CHICKEN SALAD: Omit eggs and pickles. Add 3 cups drained pineapple chunks or tidbits.

PEAS, PICKLE, AND CHEESE SALAD
(yield 25, ½ cup portions or 3¼ qts)

2 cups cheddar cheese, diced in ¼ inch
 cubes
5 #303 cans peas, drained
2¼ cups diced celery

3 cups chopped pickles
1½ cups mayonnaise
¼ cup pimiento (optional)

1. Mix cheese, peas, celery, pickles, and mayonnaise together. Add chopped pimiento if desired.

2. Cover with waxed paper and store in refrigerator to chill.

Note: Serve on lettuce leaves or shredded lettuce.

STUFFED TOMATO SALAD
(yield 25 portions)

25 washed ripe tomatoes
4½ cups chopped cabbage
2 cups chopped celery

½ cup sweet pickle relish
½ cup mayonnaise
½ tbsp salt

1. Select uniform firm ripe tomatoes.

2. Remove stem. Partially cut each tomato into 6 sections. Leave tomato uncut at bottom so that it will hold together.

3. Mix vegetables with mayonnaise and salt; place about 2 tablespoons of the mixture on each tomato.

4. Place each tomato on a lettuce leaf.

Note: 1. Serve with mayonnaise.

2. 1 qt of chicken salad or tuna salad may be substituted for the vegetables in step 3.

3. To peel tomatoes: Plunge into a large amount of boiling water for a few seconds then peel and chill.

4. 1½ qts diced cucumbers may be substituted for the cabbage and celery mixture in step 3.

RUSSIAN DRESSING
(yield 25, 1½ tablespoon portions or 2¾ cups)

2½ cups mayonnaise
6 tbsp catsup

1 tbsp worcestershire sauce
1 tbsp minced onions

1. Combine mayonnaise, catsup, worcestershire sauce, and onions. Beat 5 minutes on high speed.

2. Cover. Refrigerate until served.

CATSUP DRESSING
(yield 25, 1½ tablespoon portions or 2½ cups)

6 tbsp vinegar
1¼ cups salad oil
1¼ cups catsup
1½ tsp salt

4 tsp sugar
¾ tsp paprika
1 unbeaten egg white

1. Place vinegar, salad oil, and catsup into a mixer bowl; blend lightly.

2. Blend in salt, sugar, and paprika.

3. Add egg white and whip thoroughly.

4. Cover container, store in refrigerator to chill thoroughly.

5. Beat with wire whip before serving.

VARIATION

BLUE CHEESE DRESSING #1 : Blend 7 tbsp blue-veined cheese with the ingredients in step 1.

OLD FASHIONED LETTUCE SALAD
(yield 25, ¾ cup portions or 4¾ quarts)

1¼ gal shredded lettuce
1¼ lb chopped bacon
8 chopped, hard-cooked eggs
3 tbsp chopped onions
2 tbsp salt

pinch cayenne pepper
½ cup sugar
1½ cups cider vinegar
1½ cups melted bacon fat

1. Put 1¼ gal lettuce into roasting pan.
2. Cook bacon until crisp; drain off fat. Set fat aside for use in step 4.
3. Combine bacon and eggs; sprinkle approximately 2¼ cups of mixture over lettuce in pan.
4. Add onions, seasonings, sugar, and vinegar to bacon fat; bring to a boil.
5. Just before serving, pour approximately 2½ cups of hot vinegar mixture over lettuce in pan. Toss lightly.

HOT BACON DRESSING
(yield 25, 2½ tablespoon portions or 1 quart)

1¼ cup finely chopped onions
1¾ cup finely diced bacon
2½ cups cold water
½ cup + 2 tbsp vinegar
4 tbsp lemon juice

3 tbsp cornstarch
½ cup sugar
¾ tsp salt
¼ tsp pepper

1. Cook bacon and onions until onions are clear and bacon is crisp. Drain off and discard fat. Set bacon and onions aside for use in step 4.
2. Mix water, vinegar, lemon juice, cornstarch, sugar, salt, and pepper.
3. Heat to boiling, stirring constantly. Reduce heat, simmer 5 minutes.
4. Add onion and bacon.

Note: Pour hot dressing over shredded cabbage just before serving. Mix well.

FRUIT SLAW
(yield 25, ½ cup portions or 3 qts + ½ cup)

1¼ qts shredded cabbage
1½ qts shredded lettuce
1 cup + 2 tbsp washed, drained raisins
7½ diced, peeled oranges

2½ cups drained pineapple, chunks or
   tidbits
1½ tsp salt
¾ cup fruit french dressing

1. Combine cabbage and lettuce.
2. Add raisins, oranges, pineapple, and salt to cabbage and lettuce.
3. Just before serving add fruit french dressing. Toss lightly.

Note: See Fruit French Dressing recipe..

VARIATIONS

1. BANANA FRUIT SLAW: Substitute diced bananas for part of oranges or pineapple. Add bananas to ingredients just before serving.

FRUIT FRENCH DRESSING
(yield 25, 1½ tablespoons portions or 2½ cups).

2¼ tsp sugar
¾ tsp salt
1½ tsp paprika

1 cup salad oil
¾ cup pineapple juice
¾ cup lemon juice

1. Mix together sugar, salt, and paprika.
2. Gradually whip in salad oil and fruit juices; blend well.
3. Cover container, store in refrigerator to chill thoroughly.
4. Vigorously beat with a wire whip to incorporate well before serving over fruit salad.

THOUSAND ISLAND DRESSING
(yield 25, 1¾ tablespoons portions or 2¾ cups)

2 cups russian dressing
3 tbsp chopped green peppers
3 tbsp chopped pimiento

1 chopped hard cooked egg
3 tbsp chopped pickles or olives
1 tbsp minced onions

1. Add green peppers, pimiento, eggs, pickles or olives, and onions to russian dressing; mix together well.
2. Cover container, store in refrigerator to chill before serving.

BLUE CHEESE DRESSING #2
(yield 25, 1½ tablespoon portions or 2½ cups)

3 tbsp catsup dressing
7 tbsp blue-veined, natural cheese

⅛ tsp worcestershire sauce
2 cups mayonnaise

1. Blend catsup dressing thoroughly with blue-veined cheese and worcestershire sauce.
2. Gradually add cheese mixture to mayonnaise on low speed of mixer. Mix until thoroughly blended.
3. Cover container, store in refrigerator to chill.

SOUR CREAM DRESSING
(yield 25, 1¾ tablespoons portions or 2¾ cups)

1½ cups + 2 tbsp evaporated milk
pinch pepper
¼ cup sugar

1 tsp salt
1 cup vinegar

1. Combine milk, pepper, sugar and salt.
2. Add vinegar, gradually, stirring briskly with a wire whip until blended and sugar is dissolved.
3. Cover, store in refrigerator to chill well before serving.

Note: Mix with shredded cabbage, lettuce, or green salads.

11

SHRIMP AND CELERY SALAD
(yield 25, 1 Heaping Spoonful Portions)

2¾ qts cleaned, cooked shrimp
3¾ cups diced ½ inch pieces celery
4 tbsp lemon juice
1½ qts coarsely cut lettuce

¾ tsp salt
½ tsp pepper
1 cup salad dressing

1. Cook and clean shrimp.
2. Cut shrimp in halves or quarters.
3. Combine shrimp, celery, juice, lettuce, salt, and pepper.
4. Cover container with waxed paper, store in refrigerator to chill thoroughly.
5. Just before serving add salad dressing; toss lightly.

Note: If desired, shredded lettuce may be omitted. Serve ½ cup shrimp and celery salad in crisp lettuce cup.

CHILEAN SALAD DRESSING
(yield 25, 1½ tablespoon portions or 2½ cups)

6 tbsp minced onions
½ cup salad oil
½ cup vinegar
2 tbsp sugar

½ tsp salt
6 tbsp catsup
¾ cup chili sauce

1. Mix together onions, salad oil, vinegar, sugar, salt, catsup, and chili sauce; whip thoroughly.
2. Cover container, store in refrigerator to chill thoroughly.
3. Shake or beat well before serving.

MAYONNAISE
(yield 25, 1½ tablespoons portions or 2½ cups)

2 oz or 3 egg yolks
1⅛ tsp salt
pinch cayenne pepper
pinch dry mustard

1 tbsp + ½ tsp sugar
1¾ cups salad oil
3 tbsp vinegar

1. Beat egg yolks on high speed until light and thick, approximately 5 minutes.
2. Mix salt, cayenne pepper, mustard, and sugar together; add to beaten egg yolks and mix on high speed for 3 minutes.
3. Add oil and vinegar alternately, a little at a time, blending at high speed, approximately 7 minutes.
4. Cover container, store in refrigerator.

VARIATIONS

1. CELERY DRESSING: To 2 cups of Mayonnaise, blend in ½ cup of finely diced celery and 1¼ tsp of minced onions. Cover container and chill before serving.
2. HORSERADISH DRESSING: To 2 cups of Mayonnaise, blend in ½ cup of drained horseradish. Cover container and chill before serving.

Part Three

Poultry

STANDARD FRIED CHICKEN
(yield 24, ¼ chicken portions)

chicken, fryers, ready-to-cook, cut-up
6—2½ lb fryers
3 cups shortening, melted
1 qt sifted flour
3 tbsp salt
2¼ tsp pepper

1 tbsp monosodium glutamate
1 tbsp garlic salt
2 tsp oregano
5 eggs, whole, beaten
3 cups liquid, whole milk
1½ qts dry bread crumbs

1. Wash and clean chicken; cut each chicken in quarters.

2. Dip chicken pieces in shortening; drain.

3. Arrange chicken pieces equally in roasting pans.

4. Bake at 325 F, approximately 1 hour.

5. Remove from oven and cool.

6. Dredge chicken in flour; seasoned with salt, pepper, monosodium glutamate, garlic salt, and oregano; shake off excess.

7. Combine eggs and milk. Dip chicken in egg and milk mixture; drain.

8. Roll in bread crumbs; shake off excess.

9. Fry in deep fat (350 F) until golden brown, approximately 3 minutes.

10. Drain thoroughly, either in basket or on absorbent paper.

CHICKEN FRICASSEE
(yield 24, 1 or 2 pieces of Chicken, depending on size, and ½ cup of gravy portions)

6—3 lb fowls, chicken, ready-to-cook
1¼ cups chicken fat and melted butter
1 qt flour, sifted

3½ qts stock, chicken, hot
1¼ (14½ oz cans) evaporated milk
paprika, to garnish

1. Cut each chicken in 8 pieces. Place chickens in kettle. For 6 lb. chicken add: 1 gal water, 1 tbsp salt, 1 tsp celery salt, 1 bay leaf, and 1 tbsp monosodium glutamate. Cover.

2. Bring to a boil; reduce heat and simmer approximately 2½ hours or until tender.

3. Remove chicken, cool slightly. Bone and cut meat into ½ to 1 inch cubes. Place chicken cubes in roasting pan(s).

4. Skim off fat from stock. If necessary, add melted butter to chicken fat to make an equivalent of 1¼ cups fat.

5. Strain chicken stock; keep at 140 F or put in clean container, cover and store in refrigerator until ready to use.

6. Heat fat; blend in flour to make a roux.

7. Gradually add chicken stock and milk. Cook until thickened, approximately 10 minutes. Stir constantly.

8. Pour 2 qts sauce over chicken in each pan.

9. Bake at 350 F until thoroughly heated, approximately 25 minutes.

VARIATION

1. BROWN CHICKEN FRICASSEE: Make 6¼ cups brown gravy. Pour approximately 3 cups Brown Gravy over chicken in each roasting pan. Bake as directed in step 9.

PINEAPPLE CHICKEN
(yield 24, 2 pieces of chicken, and ¼ cup of sauce portions)

6—2½ lb chickens, fryers, ready-to-cook
1½ tsp monosodium glutamate
¼ cup soy sauce
2 tbsp salt

2 tbsp sugar
2 cups sifted flour
¼ cup soy sauce
2 #303 cans pineapple, crushed

1. Wash and clean chickens; cut each in 8 pieces.
2. Sprinkle cut side of chickens with monosodium glutamate.
3. Combine soy sauce, salt, and sugar; spread on chicken pieces.
4. Dredge chicken in flour.
5. Fry in deep fat (365 F) approximately 10 minutes.
6. Place chicken, skin side up, in each roasting pan.
7. Combine soy sauce and pineapple; spread over top of chicken in each pan.
8. Cover and bake at 350 F until chicken is tender, approximately 1¼ hours.

Part Four

Meats, Sauces and Fish

SAUERBRATEN
(yield 25, 3¾ ounce portions)

9½ lb beef, boneless, pot roast
¾ qts vinegar cider
1¼ qts water
4 #303 cans tomatoes, canned
1½ cups sugar, brown
2 tbsp salt
2 tbsp mustard, dry
1 tbsp cloves, whole

1½ tsp cinnamon
1½ tsp allspice
1½ tsp nutmeg
1½ cups onion, chopped
1½ cups celery, chopped
¾ cup + 2 tbsp carrots, chopped
1 tbsp garlic, chopped

1. Mix all ingredients and pour over meat. Cover container and store in refrigerator approximately 72 hours.

2. Remove meat from pickling solution, place meat fat side up in greased roasting pans, and brown in a 325 F oven approximately 3 hours. Turn meat frequently during cooking cycle. A meat thermometer is recommended for accuracy of doneness.

Note: 1. Use a stainless steel container for pickling solution.

2. Rare—140 F Medium—160 F Well Done—170 F

CHICKEN FRIED STEAKS
(yield 25, steak portions)

25 lbs beef, boneless, round steak
2¼ cups flour
1½ oz salt
¾ tsp monosodium glutamate
1¼ tsp pepper

¾ tsp nutmeg
2 cups milk, liquid, whole
3 eggs whole, beaten
1¼ qt bread crumbs, dry
1 cup shortening

1. Dredge steaks in seasoned flour; shake off excess.

2. Dip floured steaks in egg and milk mixture. Drain in colander.

3. Roll steaks in bread crumbs.

4. Griddle-fry steaks on greased griddle set at 350 F. Cook approximately 6 minutes on each side.

5. Serve immediately.

Note: 1 Rare—2½ minutes each side.

2 medium—4 minutes each side.

3 well done—6 minutes each side.

SEAFOOD COCKTAIL SAUCE
(yield 25, 2 tablespoon portions or 3 cups)

2 14 oz bottles catsup or chili sauce
4 tbsp vinegar
1 tbsp + 1½ tsp sugar

1 tbsp + 1½ tsp worcestershire sauce
¾ tsp salt
½ cup prepared horseradish

1. Thin catsup or chili sauce with vinegar.

2. Add sugar, worcestershire sauce, salt, and horseradish. Blend all ingredients thoroughly.

3. Cover with waxed paper and place in refrigerator to chill.

Note: If a hotter sauce is desired, add ¼ to ½ teaspoon of hot sauce in step 2.

18

SPANISH NOODLES
(yield 25, ⅞ cup (size 5 ladle) portions)

3¾ cups onions, chopped
½ cup fat
3 lb beef, ground
1½ qts or 3 #303 cans tomato puree
1¾ qts water, boiling

4 tbsp salt
1½ qt celery, chopped
1 cup peppers, green, chopped
2½ qts noodles

1. Cook onions in fat until clear.
2. Add beef and cook until meat is lightly browned.
3. Combine tomato puree, water, salt, celery, and green peppers with meat mixture, let simmer approximately 30 minutes or until celery is tender.
4. Cook noodles according to instructions on package.
5. Combine cooked noodles with tomato mixture; pour into roasting pan.
6. Bake at 325 F approximately 1 hour.

Note: 1—1 no. 10 can or 7 no 303 cans of tomatoes may be used in lieu of tomato puree in step 3; omit boiling water.

GRILLED BEEF STEAKS
(yield 25, 1 steak portions)

11¾ lbs beef, sirloin steak   shortening, melted—variable

1. Preheat griddle to 400 F and lightly grease with shortening.
2. Grill steaks on each side until desired degree of doneness is reached.
3. Serve immediately.

Note: 1. Grill approximately 2½ minutes on each side for rare; 4 minutes on each side for medium; 5 minutes on each side for well-done.
2. After grilling steaks on one side, turn and sprinkle cooked sides with a mixture consisting of 1 tablespoon garlic salt, 1 tablespoon monosodium glutamate and ½ teaspoon pepper.

SMOTHERED FRESH PORK SLICES
(yield 25, 6 ounce portions)

11¼ lb pork butts
1¼ cups flour, sifted
2 tbsp salt
½ cup fat

1 qt onions, chopped
1½ cup peppers, green, chopped
3 cups water
3 cups tomato juice

1. Trim excess surface fat from pork; cut pork into slices ½ inch thick.
2. Dredge pork slices in seasoned flour. Brown in fat. Place in roasting pans, slightly overlapping fat edge of slices.
3. Place peppers and onions on each slice.
4. Combine water and tomato juice; pour 3 cups over pork, in each pan.
5. Bake at 350 F until meat is tender, approximately 1½ hours.

SCALLOPS CREOLE
(yield 25, 1 cup portions)

2¼ cups chopped onions
1½ cups chopped green peppers
2 tbsp chopped garlic
½ cup salad oil
6⅓ #303 cans tomatoes
1 qt water
2 tbsp salt
2¼ tsp chili powder
1 tsp thyme
1¼ bay leaves

6¼ lb sea scallops
1¼ cups sifted flour
1 tbsp salt
¾ tsp pepper
1½ tsp paprika
3 large eggs, beaten whole
6 tbsp + 2 tsp liquid whole milk
2½ cups dry bread crumbs
½ cup grated parmesan cheese

1. Sauté onions, green peppers, and garlic in oil until tender.

2. Add tomatoes, water, salt, chili powder, thyme and bay leaves. Simmer about 1½ hours or until thick and glossy. Set aside for use in step 9.

3. Wash scallops thoroughly; cut large ones in half.

4. Drain well.

5. Dredge scallops in seasoned flour; shake off excess.

6. Dip in egg and milk mixture; drain in colander.

7. Roll in bread crumbs.

8. Fry in deep fat (350 F) until a light brown, approximately 3 minutes. Do not overbrown. Drain on absorbent paper.

9. Arrange fried scallops in roasting pan. Pour 1 quart of sauce over scallops. Sprinkle ½ cup of cheese over sauce.

10. Bake at 325 F for 30 minutes.

TARTAR SAUCE
(yield 25, 2 tablespoons portions)

2¼ cups salad dressing
1 cup undrained sweet pickle relish
1 tbsp finely minced parsley
3 tbsp finely chopped pimiento

1 tbsp + 1½ tsp finely minced onions
pinch of paprika
a dash of cayenne pepper

1. Combine salad dressing, pickle relish, parsley, pimiento, onions, paprika, and cayenne pepper together.

2. Cover with waxed paper. Store in refrigerator to chill well before serving.

LEMON BUTTER SAUCE
(yield 25, 3 tablespoon portions or 5 cups)

1 cup butter
¾ cup sifted flour
1⅛ tsp salt

¼ tsp pepper
1 qt boiling water
4 tbsp lemon juice

1. Melt butter. Blend in flour, salt, and pepper to make a roux.

2. Gradually add water. Cook until slightly thickened. Stir occasionally. Simmer for 10 minutes.

3. Blend in juice just before serving.

Note: SERVE OVER HOT VEGETABLES.

SAVORY CHOPPED VEAL CUTLETS
(yield 25, 1 cutlet portions)

5 lb ground veal
2 lb bulk pork sausage
½ qt dry bread crumbs

2¾ tsp salt
1 tbsp pepper
½ qt sifted flour

1. Combine veal, sausage, crumbs and seasonings.
2. Shape in 4 oz cutlets.
3. Roll cutlets in flour; shake off excess.
4. Fry in deep fat (375 F) until lightly browned, approximately 3 to 5 minutes.
5. Arrange cutlets in roasting pans. Cover pans.
6. Bake at 350 F until done, approximately 1 hour.

FRIED LIVER FINGERS
(yield 25, 4 to 6 finger portions)

7 lb beef liver
3 cups sifted flour
3 tbsp salt
1 tsp pepper

½ tsp monosodium glutamate
1 large egg, beaten whole
2 cups milk
3½ cups bread crumbs

1. Skin liver while it is partially frozen. Remove large veins and membranes. Cut into strips approximately 2½ inches long and ½ inch wide and ½ inch thick.
2. Roll liver fingers in seasoned flour.
3. Dip floured fingers in egg and milk mixture.
4. Roll fingers in bread crumbs; shake off excess.
5. Fry in deep fat (350 F) until golden brown, approximately 2 to 3 minutes.
6. Serve immediately.

Note: Bread liver fingers ahead of frying time and place on sheet pan with waxed paper separating layers; cover with waxed paper and store in refrigerator until ready to use.

OYSTERS JAMBALAYA
(yield 25, 1 cup portions or 1½ gallons)

1½ cups shortening
½ clove minced garlic
1¼ cups chopped onions
1 cup + 2 tbsp chopped green peppers
1½ cups sifted flour
1 qt oyster liquid stock or water

3¼ #303 cans tomatoes
2 tbsp salt
a pinch of cayenne pepper
6 cups chopped cooked ham
4 lb E. P.* oysters

1. Sauté onions, peppers, and garlic in shortening until soft, approximately 5 minutes.
2. Add flour to sauteed vegetables; cook for 5 minutes.
3. Add oyster liquid, tomatoes, salt, and cayenne pepper to vegetables. Cook 10 minutes, stirring occasionally.
4. Add ham and oysters. Cook slowly until edges of oysters curl, approximately 5 minutes. * See part 9.

BAKED FISH
(yield 25, 5 ounce portions)

8¾ lb halibut steak
6 tbsp lemon juice
9 tbsp melted shortening

3¾ tsp salt
1 tbsp paprika
fresh chopped parsley to garnish

1. Place single layers of fish on each greased baking sheet.
2. Cover fish on each baking sheet with the lemon juice and shortening mixture.
3. Sprinkle salt and paprika over each baking sheet of fish.
4. Bake at 375 F until brown, approximately 25 minutes.
5. Garnish with parsley before serving.

Note: 1. The amount of salt used is dependent upon the type of fish.
2. Fish is baked when it flakes easily with a fork.

BARBECUE SAUCE
(yield 25, ¼ cup portions or 1½ quarts)

1½ cups vinegar
1⅛ cups sugar
1 qt tomato puree
3 tbsp salt
6 tbsp prepared mustard
¾ tbsp cayenne pepper

½ cup ground onion
¼ cup ground green peppers
½ cup ground celery
1⅛ tsp ground cloves
1⅛ tsp ground allspice
1 tbsp + 1½ tsp chili powder

1. Mix together all ingredients.
2. Simmer 30 to 40 minutes or until vegetables are cooked and sauce blended.

Note: Use to baste meat or chicken when roasting.

CREOLE SAUCE
(yield 25, ½ cup portions or 3¼ quarts)

½ cup cornstarch
1½ cups cold water
1½ #303 cans tomatoes
2½ 6 oz cans tomato paste
2 tbsp salt
1 tsp pepper
1 tbsp sugar

¼ tsp ground cloves
¼ tsp hot sauce
2 cups ¼ inch bacon cubes
1¼ cup finely chopped onions
1¾ cup finely chopped celery
1¼ cup finely chopped green peppers

1. Mix cornstarch and cold water; cook until thickened, stirring constantly.
2. Gradually blend in hot water, whipping vigorously.
3. Add tomatoes, tomato paste, salt, pepper, sugar, cloves, and hot sauce; simmer 30 minutes.
4. Cook bacon until crisp.
5. Add onions, celery, and green peppers, sauté for 10 minutes.
6. Combine sauteed mixture with tomato sauce: cook 5 minutes longer.

Note: 1. Leftover bacon can be used.
2. Serve with omelet, macaroni, fish, or meats.

HOT MUSTARD SAUCE
(yield 25, 2 tablespoon portions or 3¼ cups)

3 cups beef broth
¾ tsp salt
a pinch of pepper
7 tbsp cornstarch
2¼ tsp sugar

4 tbsp water
4 tbsp prepared mustard
3 tbsp prepared horseradish
1 tbsp vinegar
1 tbsp butter

1. Heat broth.

2. Mix dry ingredients. Add water to make a smooth paste. Add gradually to hot broth. Stir until smooth and thickened.

3. Add remainder of ingredients. Stir until smooth.

Note: Serve with boiled beef or ham.

BEEF LOAF

(yield 25, 1 slice portion or 2 loaves)

2 qts bread crumbs
1 cup onions, finely chopped
¼ cup peppers, green, chopped
¾ cup celery, finely chopped
¼ cup shortening

7¼ lb beef, ground
4 eggs, whole, beaten
2 tbsp and 1½ tsp salt
1½ tsp pepper
¾ cup water (variable)

1. Moisten bread with water. Sauté vegetables in hot, melted shortening until light brown.

2. Combine bread crumbs, sauteed vegetables, ground beef, eggs, salt, and pepper. Mix thoroughly but lightly. Avoid overmixing, if using a mixer.

3. Add water only if necessary.

4. Shape into loaves in lightly greased roasting pan.

5. Bake at 325 F until done, approximately 1½ hours. Drain off excess fat.

VARIATIONS

1. VEAL LOAF: Omit green peppers; use 5 lbs of ground veal and 2¼ lbs of ground beef in lieu of all beef.

2. PORK LOAF: Omit green peppers; use 3¾ lb of ground lean pork and 3¾ lbs of ground beef in lieu of all beef.

3. VEGETABLE MEAT LOAF: Add 1 cup of chopped carrots to vegetables and ½ cup of catsup to meat mixture. Pour 1½ cups tomato juice over meat loaf before baking.

DRAWN BUTTER SAUCE
(yield 25, 2 tbsp portions or 3½ cups)

6 tbsp sifted flour
6 tbsp butter
3 cups boiling water

2 tbsp butter
¾ tsp salt

1. Melt butter first; stir in flour to make a roux. Add water; cook 5 minutes stirring constantly.

2. When ready to serve, add second butter and salt. Beat well.

SPAGHETTI SAUCE

(yield 25, ¾ cup portions or 4¾ quarts)

1 cup sliced canned mushrooms
4 tbsp shortening
4¾ cups chopped onions
3 tbsp dehydrated garlic
3¾ lbs finely ground beef
2 tbsp salt
4¾ #303 cans tomatoes

3½ 6 oz cans tomato paste
½ cup liquid mushroom
1¾ cups hot water
3 crumbled bay leaves
1 tbsp sugar
½ tsp cayenne pepper
¾ tsp oregano

1. Drain mushrooms and set liquid aside for use in step 2. Melt shortening; add mushrooms, onions, garlic, beef, and salt. Cook, stirring frequently, until beef is well browned.

2. Mix in tomatoes, tomato paste, mushroom liquid, water, bay leaves, sugar, cayenne pepper, and oregano.

3. Cook over low heat for 2 hours. Stir occasionally to prevent sticking. If necessary, add more hot water to keep sauce from becoming too thick.

4. Skim excess fat from sauce before serving.

MEXICANA SPARERIBS

(yield 25, 2 to 4 ribs and 2 tbsp of sauce portions)

19 lb spareribs
1 qt water
1¾ cups catsup
¾ cup soy sauce
½ cup vinegar
2 cups onions, chopped

¾ cup peppers, green, ground
6 tbsp chili powder
1 tbsp + 1½ tsp paprika
1 tbsp garlic, dehydrated
1 tbsp + 1½ tsp mustard, dry

1. Brown spareribs in 450 F oven 30 minutes; drain off excess fat.

2. Mix all remaining ingredients thoroughly. Heat sauce and pour approximately 3 cups of mixture over each pan of ribs.

3. Bake at 325 F approximately 1¾ hours, basting frequently.

4. Skim excess fat from sauce and serve sauce over spareribs.

HAMBURGERS EPICUREAN

(yield 25, 2 patties portion)

8½ lbs beef, ground
1 cup milk, evaporated
1 cup chili sauce
½ cup worcestershire sauce

2 tbsp + 1½ tsp salt
1½ tsp pepper
6 tbsp flour, sifted
1½ to 2 cups water, hot

1. Blend the first six ingredients lightly. Shape into patties weighing approximately 3 ounces each.

2. Place on baking sheets and bake at 400 F for 15 to 18 minutes.

3. Save drippings.

4. Stir flour into drippings. Add water to make 3 cups sauce or gravy. Cook for 5 minutes after gravy has thickened. Serve 1 tablespoon sauce on each patty.

Part Five

Cheese and Egg Dishes

½ #3 cyl cans tomato juice
qt whole liquid milk
:ups ground cheddar cheese

on package. Set aside for use in

hly. Add to sauteed onions; cook

Pour into two greased roasting

roasting pan of macaroni. Mix

minutes.

...ES SCALLOPED WITH CHEESE, TOMATO, AND BACON
(yield 25, 1 cup portions)

2¼ qts noodles
9¾ cups tomato puree
2¼ tsp salt
½ tsp pepper

2 tbsp sugar
3 cups ground cheddar cheese
25, ½ slices bacon

1. Cook noodles according to instructions on package. Set aside for use in step 3.
2. Combine tomato puree, salt, pepper, and sugar; heat to boiling.
3. Arrange equal amounts of noodles, tomato mixture, and cheese in layers, in each greased roasting pan.
4. Arrange bacon on top of mixture in each pan.
5. Bake at 400 F for 20 minutes or until bacon is crisp.

POTATO OMELET
(yield 25 portions)

3 qts thinly sliced, cooked potatoes
¼ cup bacon fat
25 beaten whole eggs

1 tbsp salt
1 tsp pepper
3 cups hot, whole liquid milk

1. Brown potatoes well in hot bacon fat.
2. Scale potatoes into two 9 x 13-inch roasting pans.
3. Whip eggs, salt, pepper, and milk until well blended.
4. Pour 1 qt of egg mixture over each pan of potatoes.
5. Bake at 325 F approximately 45 minutes, or until done.

Note: Serve with ham, sausage, or crisp bacon.

DEVILED EGGS

(yield 25, 2 half portions)

25 hard cooked eggs
¼ cup prepared mustard
½ tsp salt

¼ cup drained, sweet pickle relish
¾ cup salad dressing
¾ tsp paprika

1. Peel eggs and cut in half lengthwise. Carefully remove yolks and put through ricer or sieve.

2. Blend mustard, salt, pickle relish, and salad dressing with sieved yolks. Mix until smooth and creamy.

3. Fill the whites with yolk mixture, using 1 to 1¼ tbsp of filling for each egg half.

4. Sprinkle paprika on top.

5. Serve immediately or cover with waxed paper and refrigerate.

Part Six

Vegetables

GOLDEN POTATO BALLS

(yield 25, 3-1 ounce balls portions)

2½ cups dehydrated (for mashed potatoes) potatoes
½ cup nonfat, dry milk
¾ cup flour

2½ tsp salt
6¼ cups boiling water
1¼ cup flour

1. Combine potato granules, milk, flour and salt.

2. Pour water into mixing bowl.

3. On low speed, rapidly add dry ingredients. Mix until thoroughly blended, approximately 1 minute.

4. Shape mixture into balls, about 2 tablespoons each. Roll in flour.

5. Fry in deep fat (375 F) until golden brown, 1 or 2 minutes.

6. Place in a single layer in shallow pans. Roast in oven at 350 F for 5 minutes.

FRENCH FRIED ONIONS

(yield 25, 1 cup portions)

4½ lb large onions, cut into slices ¼
inch thick
water, cold—to cover
2 cups evaporated milk

1½ cups sifted flour
2½ tsp salt
a pinch of pepper

1. Separate onion slices into rings. Let stand in water 10 to 15 minutes. Drain.

2. Dip onion rings into evaporated milk; drain in colander.

3. Dredge onion rings in seasoned flour.

4. Fry in deep fat (375 F) until golden brown and tender, 5 minutes. Drain on absorbent paper.

Note: Fry in small batches as required; french fried onions lose crispness if allowed to stand.

SCALLOPED CORN

(yield 25, ½ cup portions)

½ cup melted butter or bacon fat
1½ cups crumbed crackers
2¼ tsp salt

a pinch of pepper
6 no. 303 cans cream style corn
2 cups milk

1. Blend together butter, cracker crumbs, salt, and pepper.

2. Combine corn and milk. Pour approximately 1½ qt mixture into greased roasting pan. Cover with buttered crumbs. Add remaining corn mixture; top with remaining crumbs.

3. Bake at 350 F approximately 35 minutes.

BAKED RICE MILANAISE

(yield 25, ¾ cup portions)

2½ cups rice
6 chopped, hard cooked eggs
2½ cups ground cheddar cheese
¾ tsp paprika (optional)
2¼ tsp salt

¾ cup minced onion
¾ cups minced green peppers
¾ cup + 2 tbsp shortening
6 cups tomato puree

1. Cook rice according to instructions on package.
2. Combine eggs, cheese, rice, and seasonings. Set aside for use in step 3.
3. Sauté vegetables in shortening; add to rice mixture.
4. Add tomato puree and blend.
5. Pour equally into each greased roasting pan.
6. Bake at 350 F for 25 minutes.
7. Garnish with grated cheese, if desired.

SCALLOPED SWEET POTATOES AND APPLES

(yield 25, ½ cup portions)

6¼ lb fresh, sweet potatoes
2½ qts apples, peeled, cored, cut in ½ inch slices
¾ cups + 3 tbsp packed, brown sugar

5 tbsp shortening
2¼ tsp salt
1 cup water

1. Scrub potatoes. Cover with water. Cook until tender. Drain.
2. Peel and cut into ½ inch slices.
3. Arrange potato and apple slices in alternate layers in roasting pans. Put an equal quantity in each pan.
4. Cook brown sugar, shortening, salt, and water over low heat until sugar is dissolved. Stir constantly. Pour equally over potatoes, and apples in each pan.
5. Bake at 350 F until apples are tender, approximately 1 hour.

Note: 1. 3½ lbs of apples as purchased, will yield approximately 2½ quarts, peeled and cored.

2. 5 no. 3 vacuum cans of sweet potatoes may be substituted for fresh sweet potatoes in step 3.

3. 2 tbsp cinnamon may be used in step 4 if desired.

Part Seven

Beverages

GENERAL PRINCIPLES OF COFFEE BREWING

1. Measure or weigh quantities of both water and coffee carefully. Prepare only in amounts necessary to maintain uninterrupted service. Coffee held 30 minutes or longer deteriorates in flavor and loses its aroma.

2. Use the proportion of 1 pound of coffee to 2½ gallons of water for a brew of standard strength. 3¾ cups of coffee and 7½ quarts of freshly drawn boiling water will yield approximately 25 (8 ounce) servings.

3. Ingredients for a good coffee brew are fresh coffee and freshly boiling water. Water that has been boiled a long time will have a flat taste which will be imparted to the brew.

4. For an ideal brew, boiling water should pass through coffee within 4 to 6 minutes.

5. Keep equipment clean. Clean immediately after each use to prevent the development of rancid flavors.

6. Urns and urn baskets should be washed with hot water and special urn cleaner or soda. (Do not use soap or soap powder.) Rinse with clear water. When not in use, leave 1 or 2 gallons of clear water in urn. Drain before making coffee.

7. A new urn bag should be thoroughly rinsed in hot water before using. After using, urn bags should be thoroughly rinsed in clear, cold water; keep submerged in cold water until next use.

8. Faucets and glass gauges should be cleaned often with gauge brushes, hot water, and urn cleaner or soda. Rinse with clear water. Caps on faucets and gauges are removable to permit cleaning.

COFFEE—URN METHOD

(yield 25, approximately 8 ounce portions or 6¾ qt.)

3¾ cups regular grind coffee   7½ qt briskly boiling, fresh water

1. Place wet urn bag in position. Add coffee.
2. Pour or siphon boiling water evenly over coffee.
3. Cover and let water drip through completely, in not over 6 minutes.
4. Remove urn bag immediately.
5. Draw off approximately ¼ of brew and pour back into urn to mix and insure uniformity of brew.
6. Replace cover of urn; serve.

Note: 1. If using filter method, place filter paper in dry basket carefully to avoid tearing. Distribute coffee evenly over filter paper and proceed according to Steps 2 through 6.
2. Hold finished coffee at temperature of 185 F for service.
3. Replenish water in outer jacket of urn whenever gauge shows less than half full.
4. Empty coffee grounds. Rinse urn bag thoroughly in clear, cold water; keep submerged in cold water until next use. Filter baskets should be thoroughly washed and dried.

ICED TEA

(yield 25, 1 cup portions or 1½ gallons)

1 cup + 2 tbsp loose, black tea   1 gal, + 5 cups cold water
1 qt freshly boiling water

1. Place tea in a cloth bag large enough to hold at least three times the amount.
2. Tie top of bag with cord long enough to facilitate removal. Tie cord to handle of kettle.
3. Pour the boiling water over tea bag. Cover. Steep for 5 minutes.
4. Uncover, stir, and remove bag.
5. Add tea concentrate to the cold water.

Note: 1. Do not add the cold water to the concentrate; this may produce a cloudy tea infusion.
2. The tea may be presweetened by dissolving 1½ cups of sugar in the hot concentrate before diluting with cold water.
3. If desired, cut 3 lemons into eighths to serve with the tea.

FRUIT PUNCH

(yield 25, 1 cup portions or 1½ gallons)

3 cups water   1 qt orange juice
3 tbsp loose, black tea   1 qt + 1 cup pineapple juice
2½ cups sugar   3 qts cold water
2 cups lemon juice

1. Heat water to a hard boil; pour over tea. Cover container and steep for 3 minutes.
2. Strain.
3. Add sugar; stir until dissolved.
4. Chill thoroughly.
5. Combine juices and water with chilled tea solution.
6. Cover and place in refrigerator to chill thoroughly before serving.

Note: Grape juice may be substituted for pineapple juice.

Part Eight

Pies, Cakes

and Pastry

BAKING POWDER BISCUITS
(yield 25, 2 biscuit portions)

3¼ qts sifted flour
½ qt dry, nonfat milk
6 tbsp baking powder

5¼ tsp salt
3 cups shortening
4¼ cups water

1. Mix and sift flour, milk, baking powder, and salt into mixer bowl.

2. Add shortening. Mix on low speed approximately 1 minute or until mixture resembles coarse corn meal.

3. Gradually add water and mix on low speed approximately ½ minute or until dough is just formed. DO NOT OVER-MIX.

4. Place portion of dough onto lightly floured board. Knead lightly approximately 1 minute or until dough is smooth.

5. Roll out to a uniform ½ inch thickness.

6. Cut with a 2½ inch floured cutter.

7. Arrange biscuits close together on lightly greased baking sheets.

8. Bake at 425 F 12 to 15 minutes.

Note: If time and space are limited, the dough may be cut in squares. This will eliminate re-rolling dough.

VARIATIONS

1. BUTTERSCOTCH BISCUITS: Roll dough into a rectangular sheet ⅓ inch thick. Spread with melted butter and brown sugar. Roll dough as for jelly roll. Cut into slices ¾ inch thick. Place cut side down, approximately 1 inch apart, on greased baking sheets.

2. CHEESE BISCUITS: Decrease shortening by ¼ cup. Add ½ lb (½ qt) grated cheddar cheese before adding the water. Brush with milk and sprinkle with grated cheddar cheese.

APPLE CRISP
(yield 25, ½ cup portions)

4 #2 cans sliced apples
3 tbsp lemon juice
¼ tsp grated lemon rind
4 tbsp water
1½ cups sugar
1⅛ tsp cinnamon

½ tsp nutmeg
3 tbsp cornstarch
2¼ cups sifted flour
1¾ cups packed, brown sugar
1 cup + 2 tbsp butter

1. Mix together apples, lemon juice, lemon rind, and water; scale into lightly greased 9 x 13-inch baking pans.

2. Mix together sugar, cinnamon, nutmeg, and cornstarch. Sprinkle over apples in each pan and let stand 15 minutes.

3. Blend flour, brown sugar, and butter together until crumbly. Sprinkle over apples in each pan.

4. Bake at 375 F approximately 40 to 45 minutes or until crust is formed and browned.

5. Serve hot or cold.

Note: If brown sugar is not available, granulated sugar may be substituted in step 3.

BROWNIES

(yield 25, portions)

2½ tsp salt
2¾ cups sugar
1 cup shortening
4 eggs, beaten whole
3½ cups sifted cake flour

1 cup cocoa
½ cup corn syrup
⅓ tsp vanilla
½ cup whole liquid milk
1¾ cups chopped nuts

1. Cream together salt, sugar, and shortening to a smooth dough.
2. Add eggs to creamed mixture, mix for 5 minutes.
3. Add flour and cocoa to mixture; mix well.
4. Add syrup, vanilla, milk, and nuts to mixture; mix until smooth.
5. Scale batter into two greased and floured 9 x 13 inch baking pans.
6. Bake at 350 F until done, approximately 25 minutes.
7. While still warm cut into bars.

Note: 1. Brownie bars may be rolled in confectioner's sugar, if desired, or ice as
. cake with chocolate frosting.

PEACH CRISP

(yield 25, portions)

4 #2½ cans sliced peaches
2½ cups packed, brown sugar
1 tbsp salt
2¼ cups sifted cake flour

3¾ cups rolled oats
1 tbsp + 1½ tsp cinnamon
1½ tsp nutmeg
1⅔ cups shortening

1. Drain peaches thoroughly. Set aside for use in step 6.
2. Blend together brown sugar and salt.
3. Add flour, rolled oats, cinnamon, and nutmeg to sugar; mix well.
4. Add shortening to dry ingredients; work in to form a crumbly mixture.
5. Lightly grease two 9 x 13-inch baking sheets. Scale crumb mixture into each baking pan.
6. Cover each pan with sliced peaches; top each pan with crumb mixture.
7. Bake at 375 F approximately 25 minutes or until crust is crisp.

DUTCH APPLE BREAKFAST CAKE

(yield 25 portions)

7 cups sifted flour
¼ cup baking powder
1½ tsp salt
6 tbsp sugar
1 cup shortening
3 beaten whole eggs

2¼ cups water
1 #2½ can finely chopped apples
3 tbsp melted butter
1 tbsp + 1½ tsp cinnamon
1⅔ cups sugar

1. Sift flour, baking powder and salt into mixer bowl. Add shortening and mix on low speed approximately 1 minute or until mixture resembles coarse corn meal.
2. Add eggs and water; mix until a soft dough is formed.
3. Scale batter equally into two well greased 9 x 13 inch baking pans. Spread evenly.
4. Combine apples, butter, cinnamon, and sugar. Spread over batter in each pan.
5. Bake at 400 F approximately 25 minutes.

EGG AND MILK WASH
(yield 25 portions)

3 whole eggs
1 tbsp whole, liquid milk

¼ tsp cinnamon
2 tbsp sugar

1. Mix and whip until thoroughly combined.
2. Brush on rolls or pies before baking.

Note: This wash will cover 5 to 7 pies; it may also be used as a wash for rolls.

VARIATION

1. PIE WASH: To 1 egg, slightly beaten, add ¼ cup vegetable oil and 1½ tsp baking powder. Blend. Brush top of unbaked pie crust just before baking. Use on any product calling for pie crust.

CRY BABY COOKIES
(yield 25, 2 cookie portions, or approx. 4 dozen cookies)

½ cup shortening
½ cup sugar
½ cup molasses
1 egg well beaten
3 cups sifted cake flour
1½ tsp baking powder

¾ tsp soda
1 cup shredded coconut
1 cup chopped (optional) nuts
¾ cup raisins
½ cup whole liquid milk

1. Cream shortening; add sugar, molasses, and egg. Set aside for use in Step 3.
2. Sift together flour, baking powder, and soda. Combine with coconut, nuts and raisins.
3. Add dry ingredients alternately with milk to the creamed mixture.
4. Drop approximately 1 tbsp. of dough per cookie, 2 inches apart, on greased baking sheets.
5. Bake at 375 F for 10 minutes.

Note: Corn syrup may be substituted for the molasses in step 1.

LEMON CAKE PIE
(yield 25, 6 cuts per pie portion, or 5 (9 inch) pies)

5¼ cups sugar
¾ cup butter
1½ tsp salt
13 slightly beaten egg yolks
1 cup sifted flour
5½ cups whole, liquid milk (room temp)

1¼ cups lemon juice
¾ cup ground or finely grated lemon rind
13 egg whites
5 unbaked pie shells

1. Cream sugar, butter, and salt until light and fluffy.
2. Add egg yolks to sugar and butter mixture; blend well.
3. Add flour to mixture; mix until thoroughly blended.
4. Gradually add milk, mixing on low speed until thoroughly blended. Add juice and rind.
5. Beat egg whites on high speed until they stand in stiff peaks.
6. Gently fold in custard mixture.
7. Scale approximately 3½ cups of mixture into each unbaked pie shell.
8. Bake at 350 F approximately 30 minutes.

TOMATO SPICE CAKE
(yield 25 portions)

½ cup + 2 tbsp shortening
1⅔ cups sugar
1 tbsp ground cloves
1 tbsp nutmeg
1 tbsp cinnamon
⅓ tsp salt
½ qt chopped nuts

6 tbsp soaked and drained raisins
1¾ cups tomato juice
1½ tsp soda
2 tbsp water
4¾ cups sifted cake flour
1 tbsp + ¾ tsp baking powder

1. Cream shortening, sugar, spices, and salt together one minute on low speed and three minutes on medium speed.
2. Add nuts and raisins and continue mixing.
3. Add tomato juice, then add soda which has been dissolved in water.
4. Mix and sift flour and baking powder. Add to above mixture. Mix on medium speed approximately five minutes.
5. Scale batter into 2 greased and floured 9 x 13-inch baking pans.
6. Bake at 375 F until done, approximately 25 minutes.

PECAN PIE
(yield 25, 8 cuts per pie portion or 3 to 4, 9 inch pies)

6¼ cups brown sugar
¾ cup butter
17 whole eggs slightly beaten
3⅛ cups corn sirup

1 tbsp + ¾ tsp vanilla
2¼ tsp salt
3½ cups finely chopped pecans
4 unbaked pie shells

1. Cream sugar and butter until smooth.
2. Blend in eggs.
3. Add remaining ingredients and mix until smooth.
4. Scale 3½ cups filling into each unbaked pie shell.
5. Bake at 350 F approximately 45 minutes or until filling is set.

Note: 1. Portion size is based on the extreme richness of the filling.
2. If desired, whole pecans may be placed directly on top of the filling.

BUTTERSCOTCH BROWNIES
(yield 25 portions)

2½ cups packed brown sugar
¾ cup melted butter
4 whole eggs
2¼ tsp vanilla

3 cups sifted cake flour
1 tsp baking powder
1½ tsp salt
1½ cups chopped nuts

1. Pour butter over sugar in mixer bowl. Mix on low speed until smooth and well blended. Set aside to cool.
2. Add eggs and vanilla to cool mixture in two portions, beating well after each addition on medium speed, approximately 2 minutes.
3. Sift together flour, baking powder, and salt; add to mixture and blend well on low speed, approximately 2 minutes.
4. Fold in nuts.
5. Scale batter into two well-greased 9 x 13 inch baking pans.
6. Bake at 325 F approximately 40 minutes. Do not overbake.
7. Cut into bars while warm.

DIRECTIONS FOR MAKING A ONE-CRUST PIE

BAKED PIE SHELL:

1. Make up half the recipe; divide into pieces of a size easily handled and place on a lightly floured board. Roll each piece into a cylinder approximately 3 inches in diameter, handling as little as possible. Cut each roll into five equal pieces.

2. ROLL DOUGH: Sprinkle each piece of dough lightly with flour; flatten gently. Using a floured rolling pin, roll lightly from center out to edge, in all directions, forming a circle 1 inch larger than pie pan and approximately ⅛ inch thick. Shift or turn dough occasionally to prevent sticking to board. If edges split, pinch cracks together.

3. PLACE CRUST: Fold rolled dough in half and carefully place into ungreased 9-inch pie pan. Unfold and ease into pie pan, being careful not to leave any air spaces between pan and dough. A light bounce on the board will help to eliminate trapped air.

4. REMOVE EXCESS DOUGH: Trim ragged edges approximately ½ inch beyond edge of pan. Fold extra dough back and under, and crimp with the thumb and forefinger to make a high fluted edge. Dock or prick dough on bottom and sides to prevent puffing.

5. BAKE: Bake at 450 F approximately 10 minutes or until golden brown. If available, place an empty pie pan inside of shell before baking to help prevent shrinking and puffing.

UNBAKED PIE SHELL:

1. Follow steps 1 through 4, omitting docking of dough.

2. Fill and bake in accordance with specified recipe.

DIRECTIONS FOR MAKING A TWO CRUST PIE

1. DIVIDE DOUGH: Divide dough into pieces of a size easily handled and place on a lightly floured board. Roll each piece into a cylinder approximately 3 inches in diameter, handling as little as possible. Cut into ten pieces.

2. ROLL DOUGH: Sprinkle each piece of dough lightly with flour; flatten gently. Using a floured rolling pin, roll lightly from center out to edge, in all directions, forming a circle approximately 1 inch larger than pie tin and approximately ⅛ inch thick. Shift or turn dough occasionally to prevent sticking to board.

3. BOTTOM CRUST: Fold pastry circle in half; lift onto ungreased 9-inch pie pan, with fold at center; unfold and fit carefully to eliminate air pockets; bounce lightly on board to help free trapped air.

4. FILL CRUST: Arrange approximately 3½ cups of prepared filling in lined pie pan.

5. TOP CRUST: Roll top crust in the same manner as bottom crust. Fold in half; with knife, make several slits near center fold to allow steam to escape during baking. Brush outer rim of bottom crust with water. Lay top crust over filling, with fold at center, unfold and press edges of two crusts together lightly.

6. REMOVE EXCESS DOUGH: Trim the overhanging edges of dough by pressing hands against rim of pie pan. There should be little excess dough if skill is used in gauging portions and rolling. Use dough trimmings for bottom crust only.

7. SEAL PIE: Press edges firmly together or finish crust with a fluted edge. To help prevent juice from overflowing around edges of pie, lift sealed edges of pie with edge of a knife.

8. GLAZE TOP: If a glazed top is desired, brush top with water, milk, melted butter or Egg and Milk Wash. Allow glaze to dry on pie before placing it in oven. This eliminates dark spots.

9. BAKE: Bake at 425 F approximately 45 minutes or until crust is nicely browned. The exact time will vary with the filling used in the pie. The pie is done when the juice just begins to boil out of the perforations.

VIRGINIA PASTRY
(yield 25, 3½ ounce portions or 5 pounds)

3½ cups sifted cake flour	7 tbsp compressed yeast
1½ cups sifted flour	9 tbsp sugar
7 tbsp dry, nonfat milk	2¾ cups shortening
1¾ cups water	1 tbsp + 1½ tsp salt
5 whole eggs	4½ cups sifted flour

1. Dissolve yeast in water and egg mixture; add the first three dry ingredients and mix together 2 to 3 minutes at medium speed.

2. Add sugar, shortening, salt and flour to the above, mix together in low speed for about 2 minutes. Do not overmix. Bring from mixer at 65 F or below.

3. Roll dough to ½ inch thickness. Cut with biscuit cutter or into 3 inch squares.

4. Indent center of each square with Piepin. Place 1 tbsp fruit filling in center of each square.

5. Bake at 400 F approximately 20 minutes. Cool.

Note: 1. Handling properties of the dough are best when kept cool, under 65 F.
2. This pastry dough may be used also for Coffee Cake, Biscuits, or Cinnamon Rolls.
3. 1½ *ounces* of dry yeast may be substituted for the compressed yeast in step 1.
4. Dredge cooled squares in confectioner's sugar or ice with Vanilla Water Icing.

CHERRY CRUMBLE PIE
(yield 25, 6 cuts per pie portion or 5 (9 inch) pies)

1¾ qt sifted flour	1 qt cherry juice (and water, if necessary)
2¼ tsp salt	
2¼ cups sugar	1⅔ cups sugar
1½ cups shortening	7 tbsp cornstarch
6½ #303 cans sour cherries	¼ tsp salt
1 cup, + 2 tbsp sugar	½ cup cold water
2 tbsp butter	

1. Mix together flour, salt, sugar, and shortening in a mixing bowl, on low speed to form a crumbly mixture.

2. Place 1½ cups of the mixture in each pie tin, press down firmly.

3. Drain cherries; set juice aside for use in step 6.

4. Combine cherries and sugar. Spread 2 cups of the mixture over crumbs in each pie tin. Over the cherries in each pie tin, spread 1 cup of crumb mixture. Press.

5. Bake at 375 F for 50 minutes.

6. Make a sauce; combine juice and sugar; heat to boiling point. Add cornstarch, salt, and water solution. Stir until well blended and cooked. Add butter.

7. Pour sauce over baked pies. Cool before serving.

Note: This recipe may be prepared and baked in baking sheets.

APPLE SAUCE CAKE
(yield 25 portions)

1 cup washed raisins
¾ cup hot water
2 tbsp sifted flour
⅔ cup shortening
1¾ cups sugar
⅓ tsp vanilla
3 beaten whole eggs

3¾ cups sifted flour
1 tsp cinnamon
1 tsp ground cloves
1 tbsp baking powder
1⅛ tsp soda
1½ tsp salt
2 cups + 1 tbsp applesauce

1. Cover raisins with water; allow to stand 30 minutes.

2. Drain raisins; dredge in flour and set aside for use in step 7.

3. Cream shortening, sugar, and vanilla until light and fluffy.

4. Gradually blend in eggs. Mix on medium speed until light, approximately 3 minutes.

5. Mix and sift together dry ingredients.

6. Add applesauce gradually and alternately with dry ingredients to creamed mixture. Mix on low speed approximately 1 minute or until smooth.

7. Blend in raisins.

8. Scale into 2 greased 9 x 13-inch baking pans.

9. Bake at 375 F until done, approximately 40 minutes.

PIE CRUST
(yield 25, 1/6 pie portions or 5 pies)

2 qt sifted flour
2¾ cups shortening

1½ cups (40 F to 50 F) cold water
2 tbsp salt

1. Sift flour into mixer bowl.

2. Add shortening. Mix on low speed approximately ½ minute or until mixture resembles coarse corn meal.

3. Dissolve salt in water and gradually add to flour and shortening mixture. Mix on low speed approximately 1 minute or until dough is just formed.

4. Chill dough 1 hour or longer before make-up to allow flour to hydrate and make dough easier to handle.

Note: 1. If desired 3 tbsp of sugar may be added in step 1.

2. Leftover dough may be used if kept covered in refrigerator.

VARIATION

1. TOWN AND COUNTRY CHEESE CRUST: Blend 1¾ cups coarsely ground cheddar cheese with one-fourth of pie dough. Roll out thin and cut into ½ inch slices. Use strips in lattice design as top crust for Apple Pie or Cherry Pie.

Part Nine

Miscellaneous

Information

FORMULA CONVERSION

Most of the recipes in this book are designed to produce 25 portions, and the portion size is noted in the recipe. Since there may be few occasions where you will want to serve exactly 25 people, and in some instances the acceptable size portion may be smaller or larger, it is often necessary to reduce or increase a recipe. You may adjust the recipe to yield the number of servings needed, or to use the amount of ingredients available, or to produce a specific number of smaller servings.

1. To adjust to yield a specific number of servings;

First—Obtain a working factor by dividing the number of servings needed by 25.

For example:

73 (servings needed) ÷ 25 = 2.92 Working Factor

Then—Multiply the quantity of each ingredient by the working factor.

For example:

1.5 lb (recipe) × 2.92 Working Factor = 4.38 lb (quantity needed)

The part of the pound is converted to ounces by multiplying the decimal by 16.

For example:

.38 lb × 16 ounces = 6.08 ounces

After the part of the pound has been converted to ounces, use the following scale to "round off";

.10 to .12 = 0
.13 to .37 = ¼ ounce
.38 to .67 = ½ ounce
.68 to .87 = ¾ ounce
.88 to .99 = 1 ounce

Thus 6.08 ounces will be "rounded off" to 6 ounces and 4 lb 6 ounces will be the quantity needed.

2. To adjust the recipe on the basis of a quantity of an ingredient to be used;

First—Obtain a Working Factor by dividing the pounds you have to use by the pounds required to yield 25 servings.

For example:

32 lb ÷ 10 (lb per 25 serving) = 3.20 Working Factor

Then—Multiply the quantity of each ingredient in the recipe by the working factor.

3. To adjust to yield a specific number of servings of a specific size.

First—Divide the desired portion size by the standard portion of the recipe.

3 oz (desired size) ÷ 4 oz (standard portion) = .75

73 (servings needed) × .75 = 54.75

54.75 ÷ 25 = 2.19 Working Factor

Then—Multiply the quantity of each ingredient in the recipe by the Working Factor.

FORMULA CONVERSION

Portion control is ensured when the correct **size** serving utensil is used. See Equivalent Table for weights and measures, page 49.

TEMPERATURES AND TESTS FOR STAGES OF SUGAR COOKERY

STATE	TEMPERATURE	TESTS	USES
Thread	230 to 234 F 110 to 112 C	Sirup spins a 2 inch thread when dropped from fork or spoon.	Cooked icings
Soft ball	234 to 240 F 112 to 115 C	Sirup forms a soft ball when dropped into cold water. Ball flattens on removal.	Fudge, Fondant, Penoche
Firm ball	244 to 248 F 118 to 120 C	Sirup becomes a firm ball when dropped into cold water. Ball does not flatten when removed.	Carmels
Hard ball	250 to 266 F 121 to 130 C	Sirup forms a ball when dropped into cold water, hard enough to hold its shape, yet plastic.	Divinity, popcorn balls, marshmallows
Soft crack	270 to 290 F 132 to 143 C	Sirup separates into threads when dropped into cold water. Threads are hard but not brittle.	Butterscotch taffies
Hard crack	300 to 310 F 149 to 154 C	Sirup separates into threads which are hard and brittle when dropped into cold water.	Brittle glace
Barley sugar	320 F or 160 C	Thick clear liquid.	
Carmel	338 F or 170 C	Barley sugar becomes brown.	Flavoring and Color

TEMPERATURE RANGE FOR OVENS

DESCRIPTION	TEMPERATURE	BROWNING TESTS
Very slow Slow	250 to 300 F 325 F	Paper turns delicate brown in 5 minutes.
Moderate	350 to 375 F	Paper turns golden brown in 5 minutes.
Moderately hot Hot	400 F 425 to 450 F	Paper turns deep brown in 5 minutes.
Very hot	475 to 500 F	Paper turns dark brown in 3 minutes.

Note: Unglazed white paper should be used to make the browning test. White flour may be used to make the same test.

RECIPE ABBREVIATIONS

A. P.—as purchased   pt —pint

E. P.—edible portion   qt —quart

tsp —teaspoon   gal—gallon

tbsp —tablespoon   oz —ounce

—number   lb —pound

    Unless otherwise specified in the ingredients listing, the E. P. weight is used for all recipes in this book.

EQUIVALENT TABLE FOR WEIGHTS AND MEASURES

TSP	TBSP	OUNCES	CUPS	SCOOPS	LADLES	FLUID MEASURE	LB WEIGHT
¾	¼						
3	1	½					
	2	1	⅛	1-#30			
	4	2	¼	1-#16	size 1		
	5	2½	⅓	1-#12			
	6⅔	3½—4	⅖	1-#10			
	8	4	½	1-# 8	size 2		
	10	5	⅔		size 3		
	12	6	¾		size 4		
	14	7	⅞		size 5		
	16	8	1			½ pt	
	18	9	1⅛		size 6		
		12	1½			¾ pt	
		16	2			1 pt	1 lb
		24	3			1½ pt	
		32	4			1 qt	
		64	8			2 qts	4 lb
		128	16			1 gal	8 lb

CONVERSION TABLES FOR FOREIGN EQUIVALENTS

DRY INGREDIENTS

Ounces		Grams	Grams		Ounces	Pounds		Kilograms	Kilograms		Pounds
1	=	28.35	1	=	0.035	1	=	0.454	1	=	2.205
2		56.70	2		0.07	2		0.91	2		4.41
3		85.05	3		0.11	3		1.36	3		6.61
4		113.40	4		0.14	4		1.81	4		8.82
5		141.75	5		0.18	5		2.27	5		11.02
6		170.10	6		0.21	6		2.72	6		13.23
7		198.45	7		0.25	7		3.18	7		15.43
8		226.80	8		0.28	8		3.63	8		17.64
9		255.15	9		0.32	9		4.08	9		19.84
10		283.50	10		0.35	10		4.54	10		22.05
11		311.85	11		0.39	11		4.99	11		24.26
12		340.20	12		0.42	12		5.44	12		26.46
13		368.55	13		0.46	13		5.90	13		28.67
14		396.90	14		0.49	14		6.35	14		30.87
15		425.25	15		0.53	15		6.81	15		33.08
16		453.60	16		0.57						

LIQUID INGREDIENTS

Liquid Ounces		Milliliters	Milliliters		Liquid Ounces	Quarts		Liters	Liters		Quarts
1	=	29.573	1	=	0.034	1	=	0.946	1	=	1.057
2		59.15	2		0.07	2		1.89	2		2.11
3		88.72	3		0.10	3		2.84	3		3.17
4		118.30	4		0.14	4		3.79	4		4.23
5		147.87	5		0.17	5		4.73	5		5.28
6		177.44	6		0.20	6		5.68	6		6.34
7		207.02	7		0.24	7		6.62	7		7.40
8		236.59	8		0.27	8		7.57	8		8.45
9		266.16	9		0.30	9		8.52	9		9.51
10		295.73	10		0.33	10		9.47	10		10.57

Gallons (American)		Liters	Liters		Gallons (American)
1	=	3.785	1	=	0.264
2		7.57	2		0.53
3		11.36	3		0.79
4		15.14	4		1.06
5		18.93	5		1.32
6		22.71	6		1.59
7		26.50	7		1.85
8		30.28	8		2.11
9		34.07	9		2.38
10		37.86	10		2.74

Index

52